Get In
A Good Mood
& Stay There

DANNIE DE NOVO

Foreword by BOB PROCTOR • Afterword by TROY DUNN

Published by
Hasmark Publishing
www.hasmarkpublishing.com

Copyright © 2018 Dannie De Novo
First Edition

No part of this book may be reproduced or transmitted in any form or by any means, electronic or mechanical, including photocopying, recording or by any information storage and retrieval system, without written permission from the author, except for the inclusion of brief quotations in a review.

Disclaimer

This book is designed to provide information and motivation to our readers. It is sold with the understanding that the publisher is not engaged to render any type of psychological, legal, or any other kind of professional advice. The content of each article is the sole expression and opinion of its author, and not necessarily that of the publisher. No warranties or guarantees are expressed or implied by the publisher's choice to include any of the content in this volume. Neither the publisher nor the individual author(s) shall be liable for any physical, psychological, emotional, financial, or commercial damages, including, but not limited to, special, incidental, consequential or other damages. Our views and rights are the same: You are responsible for your own choices, actions, and results.

Permission should be addressed in writing to Dannie De Novo at dannie@danniedenovo.com

Editor: Sigrid Macdonald
Book Magic
http://bookmagic.biz

Book Layout: Anne Karklins
anne@hasmarkpublishing.com

ISBN 13: 978-1-989161-43-2
ISBN 10: 198916143X

For my daughter, Carson…
All my love,
All day, every day;
Always and from everywhere I am to everywhere you go.

Follow your heart, Baby,
and the rest will follow you.

TABLE OF CONTENTS

Foreword — 7

PART I: Get in a Good Mood

Introduction — 11

Chapter 1: You Are Here — 13

Chapter 2: Start Your Engines (It Starts with You) — 17

Chapter 3: Where the Rubber Meets the Road (Desire, Decision & Action) — 21

Chapter 4: Don't Ride Your Brakes (Let Go of Attachments) — 25

PART II: Stay in a Good Mood

Chapter 5: All Aboard (Turn Your Focus Toward Others) — 31

Chapter 6: All Roads Lead to Rome (Spirituality) — 37

Chapter 7: Get a Move On (Exercise) — 41

Chapter 8: Travel Companions (Find the Like-Minded) — 45

Chapter 9: Put Yourself on the Map (Your Self-Image) — 49

Chapter 10: Put the Wind Back in Your Sails (Daily Rituals and Self-Care) — 55

Chapter 11: Tour of Duty (Teach This Stuff to Others) — 63

Chapter 12: Rite of Passage (Pay Close Attention to Your Habits) — 67

Chapter 13: Blaze a Trail (Be an Unbridled Dreamer) — 71

Chapter 14: A Seasoned Traveler (My Faith in You) — 75

Aferword — 79

FOREWORD

Having focused my life's work on one thing for over a half of a century, I can assuredly say that I better understand some things in my field that the average individual would or could easily miss.

I have been in the Personal Development field for well over fifty years and have worked all over the world. My company has impacted the lives of millions of people in many different cultures, so I'm confident in saying that I have a pretty good idea of what this book is about. On top of that, the author is a dear friend of mine and I have had the pleasure of watching her do what she is sharing with you.

Dannie is the real deal. That may seem like a bold statement; however, given that eighty percent of the people who are teaching have never done what they are teaching, I can tell you that she speaks with conviction. She has done and is doing what she is sharing with you in this book.

Dannie De Novo has captured the essence of a very important subject everyone can learn and benefit from. "How to Get in a Good Mood & Stay There." You have to admit, that's a pretty cool idea.

You might be saying to yourself – no one stays in a good mood all of the time. You might be right BUT there are people you know who you rarely, if ever, see in a bad mood. Being in a good mood is a choice and can become a habit; it is seldom something that just happens. To get in a good mood and to stay there requires a working knowledge of the Mind; a clear understanding of why we do what we do and why we don't do many things we want to do.

Make a decision that you are not only going to read this book, but you are going to study it. Treat it as a guide to really living life to the fullest. You can have the things you want and you will have them when you act on the ideas Dannie is sharing and make them a way of life.

Each time you pick up this book, before you start reading, sit quietly and let your mind wander. Think of how good everything looks when you are in a good mood; it makes for such a beautiful picture.

All of the really successful people I know are always in a good mood. They do not permit the problems of the day to determine their mood. They set and achieve one goal after another and live exciting, dynamic lives. They expect success and they get it. You can too.

Bob Proctor
Master Success Coach
Best-selling Author of *You Were Born Rich*.

Dannie De Novo

PART I
GET IN A GOOD MOOD

INTRODUCTION

"You can't use an old map to explore a new world."
~ Albert Einstein

Commit to charting a new course.

I had some trouble writing this book. You see, dear reader, I don't see myself as someone with a lot to say. I do, however, see myself as someone who has experienced some of life's lessons and a number of detours, and as a result of those experiences, I can now listen to others and offer some wisdom, compassion and, if need be, some refuge.

Long ago, when I sat down to write, the words would pour onto the paper like my tears into my bath water most nights. It was natural – the words came out naturally – much like my bathroom tears. I spent a lot of time imprisoned by a poor mood. It was more than a poor mood or even a really bad mood, in fact. It was a severe – what I term – spiritual depression.

Miraculously, or so I thought at the time, I managed to eventually escape from the desperate grips of my depression. I got to the point where I even thought I was doing fairly well. Then one day, the task of writing this book was given to me, and when I sat down to write it, I realized that I did not have a systematic approach for getting in a good mood, and well, staying there. I wanted to develop a good mood roadmap that was easy to follow, both for myself and for others.

The purpose of this book is nothing more than to bring a little awareness to those out there who are searching for the same answers for which I have searched. Life is a journey, not a destination. So, too, is getting into a good mood and staying there. It is a process and it requires some trial and error, some fortitude, and lots of help from lots of lovely souls along the way.

What I have strived to do within these pages is show you the course I have taken to shift my attitude and find my good mood. I think, with any goal, it helps to start with some semblance of a plan. I'll show you how to navigate the bumps in the road, and you, dear reader, you get to decide where your "happiness X" marks the spot.

I wish you an amazing and successful journey, dear reader. May you draw your own map and may you find and hold on to your good mood.

> "All you need is the plan, the road map,
> and the courage to press on to your destination."
>
> ~ *Earl Nightingale*

CHAPTER 1

You Are Here

"There is no way to happiness… happiness is the way."
~ *Thich Nhat Hahn*

Destination: Your Good Mood!

Population: 1 (…but many others will follow your lead!)

Elevation: Yep!

Visibility: Your Amazing Future and Perpetual Good Mood Ahead!

Fun Fact: Your Good Mood Is Habitual

Hey there, my dear reader! How are you today? Are you in a good mood?

What if I told you that your good mood is just right around the corner? What if I said that you can get to your good mood by way of these pages and hold on to it for days, weeks, months… even years into the future?

I mean, what good ever came out of being in a bad mood? Have you ever nailed a job interview or scored a hot date when you were in a bad mood? No! Ever eaten a healthy meal or taken good care of yourself when you were in a bad mood? Of course not!

Within these pages a very special map exists to help you find your good mood and stay there. There is an amazing treasure out there with your name on it, but there is a lot of bad mood terrain to navigate through to attain it. You may be here today, yes, but you do not need to stay in this same place tomorrow. You have the power to change your mood!

This book will serve as your compass. When you lose sight of your good mood, don't haphazardly search for it. Let this book serve as your guide and get you back on course.

Your mood, your attitude is habitual. The path you are on right now is mostly directed by your habits. You, my dear reader, are running around on cruise control and you don't even realize it. It's kind of a crazy concept to entertain, but once you see what getting off autopilot can do for you, you will never want to turn it back on.

You can change those bad mood habits, one by one, so that you don't constantly ride around in circles. You have the ability to take yourself from where you are to where you want to be. Don't throw away another day to the pain of feeling sad, depressed, lonely, angry, bitter or just plain numb. You should be enjoying your life and I want to help you make that enjoyment a priority.

Throughout our time together, I will lead you toward your good mood and give you the keys to keeping it. You will uncover your life's passion, discover a deep sense of gratitude within, connect with your soul and learn ways to spread that good mood of yours to others!

So, pull over and kick that bad mood to the curb. Let's get you focused on the horizon ahead! I am so excited for you and I am so excited to share with you the steps I took to get in a good mood and stay there!

You know, when I was in a bad mood, I didn't particularly like my behavior. When I was in a bad mood, I tended to isolate myself. I didn't reach out to people and talk to them. I certainly didn't try to find out more about them. When I was in a bad mood, I sped and took greater chances on the road. Red lights were more like yellow lights and stop signs more like yield signs. When I was in a bad mood, I did not think at my optimal level. My problem-solving abilities were decreased. When I was in a bad mood, my daughter did not want to play with me. When I was in a bad mood, I ate pizza, s'mores, ice cream, fried foods and spaghetti – all at the same time. When I was in a bad mood, I drove by (no, sped past) the gym with my middle finger out the window. When I was in a bad mood, I was careless with money. When I was in a bad mood, I treated myself poorly.

Why, oh why, then would anyone ever allow himself or herself to be in a bad mood? As I mentioned a little earlier, it comes down to one simple word. *Habit*. For the longest time, being in a bad mood was a habit of mine. I did it automatically, like applying the car brake when seeing a stop sign ahead. I just accepted that this was who I was – I wasn't a happy person. I identified with the blatant sarcasm and snarkiness that enveloped my life. In fact, I did this to the extreme during more than one depressive episode. Each time, I blamed everything and everyone for why my life was so crappy all the time. I had plenty of excuses for being in a bad mood and I believed every single one of them. And each time, I had to wake myself up and force myself to realize that I was the reason my life sucked, and that was a jagged little pill to swallow.

We need to develop a little awareness of these bad mood habits so that we change them, one at a time, and not allow ourselves to constantly give into those feelings of negativity. I'm not gonna lie – changing these habits can be hard. It was hard for me. It still is hard sometimes. But riding out life in a 1997-model Ford pickup truck with a rusted-out bed isn't going to do it for you anymore. The miles are getting high; there are some dings and dents you aren't proud of; and you are leaking oil. I am guessing you want more. I am guessing you want some precision, a little more torque and a whole lotta horsepower behind you. It's time for an upgrade.

Trade in that clunker for the sports car of your choice and buckle up, because baby, once you upgrade your system, it's going to be a sweet, sweet ride!

> "There are only two mistakes one can make along the road to truth; not going all the way, and not starting."
> ~ *Buddha*

CHAPTER 2

Start Your Engines (It Starts with You)

"It's your road, and yours alone. Others may walk it with you, but no one can walk it for you."
~ Rumi

You alone are the answer.

You are in the driver's seat – you hold the keys to your good mood. No outside events, people, circumstances or situations are responsible – only you.

You have to suck in your gut and pull on your big girl panties to accept the following statement: Everything you are experiencing in your life is due to your thoughts. No one else is to be blamed (or congratulated) for your current life.

I think this concept hit me like the smell of hot asphalt in the summer when I realized that I could no longer blame my parents, my upbringing, my current relationships or my genetics for my depression or anything else negative in my life. It was all on me. That realization, while very difficult to admit to myself, was also very freeing.

The good news, my beloved reader, is that once you accept that you and you alone are responsible for who you are, where you are and what you are, you also ultimately realize that you (and you alone) have the power to change these manifestations. To start this process, I shifted my perspective from blame of everyone else and turned my focus inward. And once that occurred, I quickly realized there was something that I needed to address before moving forward.

This leads us to the first mile marker on this journey – forgiveness. You have to let go of the past. Forgive yourself.

Not so long ago, I carried great shame, guilt and embarrassment about my depression. In fact, very few people even knew what had happened to me. I could not relive the story in my mind let alone say it out loud. I had a lot to let go of, and it wasn't easy for me. There was a part of me that was convinced that given everything I had been through and given everything I had put other people through, I deserved to pay a penance. I did not deserve forgiveness – not even from myself. That was horribly ignorant thinking on my part. All I was doing was propagating more of the same.

If you are constantly dwelling on a state of mind, you become that state of mind. When I was young, I got into a pattern of bad thinking, probably because I wasn't feeling fulfilled and wanted more from life and was constantly told there wasn't any more than what was right in front of me. I had questions about purpose and meaning and life. These questions were fine, but where I erred was in sitting with my feelings of frustration, guilt, anger and the sense of unworthiness I held. I should have recognized the emotions, taken note of the information they were giving me, and then let them go.

So, your first order of business, make the decision to forgive yourself, and then… actually… forgive… yourself. You were doing the best you could, given your set of circumstances, the amount of support you had and your level of understanding and insight at the time. That person from the past no longer exists. You are here today, with the added benefit of increased wisdom and resources. So, give the past you a break and forgive that older version of yourself.

My theory is this – if you learned a lesson in the process, then you are deserving of your own forgiveness, even if no one else will grant forgiveness to you.

The second mile marker is to accept where you are today – right this very minute. You must accept the present reality for what it is – simply a moment in time. Stop comparing today with the benchmark for where you *should* be. You are where you are today because of past thinking (past thinking that you have since forgiven yourself for). So, in essence, who you are today is a reflection of the former you – the you you are about to leave in the past once and for all. It is fine to make some mental notes about where you are now, but you cannot become hung up on a fleeting moment in time. You have to start directing your energy to where you want to go.

Take note of how you are feeling. Acknowledge it, but don't judge it. Let it go. There is no reason to keep a death grip on any negative (or, honestly, positive) emotion. Trust me, emotions are like subway trains during rush hour – another one will be along the way shortly.

> "Happiness is not something ready made.
> It comes from your own actions."
>
> *~ Dali Lama*

CHAPTER 3

Where the Rubber Meets the Road (Desire, Decision & Action)

"Forget about the fast lane. If you really want to fly,
just harness your power to your passion."
~ *Oprah Winfrey*

Fear is a funny thing.

Fear is capable of being both an incredible motivator and an incredible hindrance. The only other force on earth that I have experienced like this is love. Luckily for all of us, love can trump fear. So, too, can desire if you use it properly.

By virtue of your decision to get into a good mood, you are committing to a number of things. All these things will be changes, and regardless of whether you are the instrument of your own changes or not, your bad mood habits are going to fight like a stunt driver at a monster jam truck rally to keep things at status quo. This is why change is so difficult. Your brain and your body are used to your bad mood, so they will do everything they can to maintain that sense of familiarity. How do you get around this ingrained programming? You bring your focus back to your desire to make the change and, when you encounter fear and frustration, the process repeats itself.

Desire begets decision; decision begets action; action circles back to desire and the cycle repeats itself until you reach your desired goal. This cycle is the means I used to combat fear and shift my attitude. This cycle is part of how I get into a good mood and stay there.

For me, it's a lot like learning how to ride a horse. At the beginning, the horse dictates your path, and you basically just sit there. Then, as you get more comfortable, you take some chances, and inevitably fall off. Then you get scared, so you let the horse take over again. Then you get mad because you are tired of the horse running your leg into trees, so you try and manhandle the horse. The result? You fall off again. I mean, you can't out-muscle an 1100-pound animal. So, you compromise and you and the horse start to work together toward your desired goal. The funny thing about horseback riding is, though, the longer you ride, regardless of how good you get, you still fall off sometimes. It's the law of averages. Any time that you put your foot in the stirrup and mount up, there is that chance that your butt will hit the dirt, so be prepared.

One night, I was riding a beautiful, big bay of mine named Apollo. Apollo was a big boy and he liked to buck. A buck is when a horse lowers its head and kicks up its hind legs and hind quarters into the air. He was always pretty spirited and was guilty of often-times finding excuses to misbehave. This night was one of those nights. He saw some children playing nearby and took his chance. He bucked so hard that I came up straight out of the saddle. My feet completely came out of the stirrups. The funny part was that I came straight back down, and luckily for me, Apollo hadn't moved. Well actually, he moved just a bit. He moved just enough that I landed almost directly on the horn of the Western saddle I had elected to ride in that night. (Why, oh why, didn't I go English!?) Anyway, my pubic bone came into direct contact with the silver-encrusted horn of the saddle, and it hurt. I mean, it really, really hurt. It hurt so badly that I just slid off the side of my horse on to the ground from sheer pain.

I lay there for a minute and tried to get up. When I rolled onto my knees, it became apparent that a crowd had now gathered around us to see what happened. It also became painfully obvious that the sudden impact with the saddle had caused my jeans to explode open, starting at the zipper and going all the way down to my knee. How lucky I was to have chosen purple underwear that day.

I mustered up as much dignity as I could find and stood up to get back on. Everyone just stood there and watched me struggle in pain to get back on my horse. Then I had to do the ride of shame back to my barn with essentially no pants.

By the time we got back to the barn, I had a dark bruise that ran from my left knee all the way to my chest. And I mean, it was the darkest purple you have ever seen, even darker than my exposed purple underwear. I developed a massive hematoma in an awkward place, but other than that, I was just heavily bruised and heavily embarrassed.

Yes, I've had a few epic falls off the horse. I've had a few epic falls – I've had a few epic fails. Actually, I screw up big sometimes. Really, really big. But, I still have to get back on that horse. I can't lie in the middle of some field forever while people laugh at the fact that my pants seem to have disappeared.

How do you keep getting back on a horse that bucked you so hard you aren't sure if you will ever have children? Shift your attitude. First, forgive your mistake. Then, find your desire. You have to have the desire to get back on your Apollo, whatever that means to you at the time. You have to want to ride that crazy steed. You've got to want it so badly that even a three-foot-long body bruise won't keep your butt out of that saddle. Then, you decide to get back in that saddle, and you commit to staying there. And then, most importantly, you mount up.

Above all else, YOU MUST ENJOY THE RIDE! You cannot sit up there and wait for the next buck. You can't constantly brace yourself for pubic-bone impact. You can't continue to relive the night your pants exploded. You need to relax and enjoy the fresh air, the sounds of nature, your quirky horse. Enjoy being in the moment and being alive. And when the next buck comes, and it will come sooner or later, just know that you have the strength to withstand it. You may blow open your jeans, you may have to tell your OB-GYN a bizarre story, you may even be sidelined for a few days so that you can let your purple body heal, but you will survive – because of your attitude. And then, one day, the incident becomes a funny story you tell people you have just met randomly at your office holiday party.

Life is so much more fun when you don't care that everyone can see your purple underwear. Life is so much more fun when you let it actually be *fun* – when you set your attitude to a higher frequency… and, yes, when you can laugh at yourself from time to time.

Let go of the fear, and instead, ride on toward your desire. Ride hard; ride often; enjoy the ride!

> "Press forward. Do not stop, do not linger in your journey, but strive for the mark set before you."
> ~ *George Whitefield*

CHAPTER 4

Don't Ride Your Brakes (Let Go of Attachments)

"I can't change the direction of the wind, but I can adjust my sails to always reach my destination."
~ Jimmy Dean

Unattach yourself.

While I have been writing this section, spring is in the air. It's light out a little later in the day. The birds are busy and singing early in the morning. The squirrels are running around again. There are little tiny buds on some of the trees. My horse Huck is shedding his winter coat. Never mind the fact that it has still been snowing occasionally. The point is – spring is *expected*. I *expect*, that one day soon, I will be able to walk out of my house and not have to wear three layers of clothes. And, even though I am still scraping ice off my windshield from time to time, I am *attached* to this idea of winter coming to an end. And, based upon the behavior of the plants and animals around me, I am not the only one living in this expectation.

I think we often live a lot of our lives this way – focusing on the expectation of future events rather than living in the here and now.

I also think, given our society today, we often place a lot of weight on what the future will bring us. Sometimes, expectation can be a good thing. Like, expecting spring and summer. It gives us hope of warm days, sunshine, playing outside again, swimming, picnics. And, we can say with a great deal of certainty, that spring *will* come eventually, even if it is a little later than we would like.

When we get ourselves into trouble with expectation is when we are constantly looking toward the future, waiting for future events to bring us… something. Happiness, something new, the idea of something different. How often do you think to yourself something along these lines… "I'll be happy when summer is here. I'll be happy when summer is over and the kids go back to school. I'll be happy when I get that new job. I'll be happy when I make more money. I'll be happy when I can move away from here. I'll be happy when I lose five pounds. I'll be happy when I get married. I'll be happy when I have a baby. I'll be happy when this (whatever "this" is) is over"?

Since we cannot find happiness within and with the here and now, we place it on some future event or ideal and attempt to convince ourselves that we only need to achieve this milestone or reach a certain life destination and all will be as we hoped. The problem is this: summer comes and goes, with no real change in us. Or, we continue to fight every rung of that corporate ladder, each one harder to step onto than the one below it. But, when we climb up high on that ladder, we find not much has changed. Our level of happiness is about the same.

I spent a fair amount of my life waiting and hoping that future events would turn out a certain way – expecting that things would change in the future. For a while, it was a survival mechanism. When I was young and depressed, and quite honestly, very ignorant about how life worked, I was banking on the fact that things would get better as I got older. I thought that I would feel better when I graduated from high school and went to college or when I moved away from home. And, yes, at first, things did feel better. But that feeling was a fleeting moment in time.

The problem was that I had not done any self-awareness work. I was expecting my happiness would reveal itself in something external to myself. And, I don't know that expectation is so much the culprit here as is the idea of attachment. We become attached to certain outcomes, and if things don't turn out as planned, then we end up struggling with life because the eventual outcome did not meet that expectation to which we were so heavily attached.

To constantly be attached to some future outcome leaves you living your life in a time where you have no control and within a time that does not yet exist. You are missing today. You are missing your life as it is, right now, right in front of you. If you are trying to escape the current version of you, as I once was, then living in the future is a great way to do it. It is also a fantastic way to breed more displeasure, unhappiness and self-contempt. And while I agree that we need to dream, to push ourselves out of our comfort zones to grow, I do not think we can grow until we are firmly rooted in the present. That is why loving ourselves, in the present moment, is so important. This is why gratitude is so important.

I think, that if we come to *expect* consistent love of and from ourselves, then we can reach those lofty dreams of ours one day. And let's face it, if you are going to be attached to anything in this world, it might as well be yourself. So, let go of those attachments and start relying on yourself. Your relationship with self is going to last a long, long time.

"The essence of the Way is detachment."
~ *Bodhidharma*

PART II
STAY IN A GOOD MOOD

CHAPTER 5

All Aboard
(Turn Your Focus Toward Others)

"A journey is best measured in friends,
rather than miles."
~ Tim Cahill

Don't dwell on a bad mood; turn your focus toward helping others.

Yes, at one point, I had a lot of work to do on myself. (But, then again, I will always be working on making me better and happier!) For me, at the time, I was still struggling with a higher sense of purpose and I wanted to feel a deeper sense of connectedness. This is where my personal spirituality practice came in. For desire to be present within me, I must be connected to a higher purpose. I must be connected at a higher level. If I am not connected to spirit, to the Universe, then I have no fire burning within, no reason to put forth more than minimal survivor-level effort into anything.

I am not speaking here of religion. If God serves this purpose for you, then by all means, connect with God. I grew up with a strict Roman Catholic upbringing, and so for me, thinking in terms of God alone tends to bring negative images. So, my image of God is more like the entire Universe, working together as one powerful and majestic force that dictates all that ever was and all that will ever be. It is this omnipotent power I speak of when I say I attempt to connect with or tap into a higher state.

I know that I am part of the Universe, and as such, I have inherent power within. However, I also know that I am not capable of manifesting so much as a nickel without the help of the Universe. In order for me to create anything – a state of mind, a trip across the globe, a baby – my energy must collide into and unite with the energy of the abundant Universe. There is no other possible way for absolutely anything to ever happen. In short, in order to gain, I must give.

When life appears to be handing me nothing but undesirable results, I know only one thing could have occurred. I am focused too much on the talk going on inside of my head and not enough on others. So now, I try to focus most of my work on other people. Every morning I ask the Universe what I can do to help others and I ask that I am alert and aware when others are seeking my help in any way. I ask to have a voice that resonates with others so that they hear (or read) what they need.

I once believed that the only way I could help others was to have an advanced degree in some area. Now I know that I help so many people just by listening to them and acknowledging what they are going through may be hard for them. I try not to judge but to support. I try to be understanding and open-minded.

I honestly think the major lesson to be learned from my depression was a lesson in compassion – to truly understand suffering of the mind and spirit so I could relate to others experiencing the same kind of things. When I see that look of confusion or desperation in the eyes of another, I want nothing more than to help him or her heal his or her heart. I listen and try to respond in a meaningful way.

Moreover, with respect to connecting with others, I challenge you to find a better mood than that attributed to being in love. I am not speaking of just romantic love, here. I fell in love with my daughter the first moment her pissed-off, little scowled-face looked me right in the eye and seemed to say, "Are you kidding me right now?" Funny as that was, I actually recognized that face – it was an expression I sometimes used. She and I were soulmates from the beginning.

Positive human interaction – love, in any form – is the foundation of a good mood. Little to no positive human interaction leads you straight to a bad mood. Let me explain further.

My family was not a group of huggers. We didn't really show much physical affection toward one another. I never realized how closed off we were until I befriended a woman who liked to hug. One day, when she was saying good-bye to me, she reached out for a hug and lightly touched my back and said, "I will just give you a little hug. I know they make you uncomfortable." Uncomfortable! She thought I was uncomfortable?! Here I was thinking what a good job I had done by even engaging in a hug with her, which was so foreign to me. It was then that I realized how much I had been cheated. These days, I try to be a good hugger. Some days it still feels a little weird for me, but what I can say about hugging is this: when I look around and see the richest people in the world, meaning those who live a truly amazing and fulfilling life, those people are always engaged in human interaction. They are huggers. They are sharers. They embrace themselves. They are open to others.

Don't miss out on those hugs. They are necessary for the survival of the species and for the survival of your good mood. There is a reason that the need for human interaction and connection is hard-wired into our brains. There is a reason human touch and the desire for sex is a biological need. We cannot exist on our own. The Universe operates under the premise that energy is feeding off and interacting with other energy. If there is only one energized entity, it cannot react against or toward anything else. Everything becomes stagnate. Our thoughts and our feelings are energy and radiate out to others. Likewise, others' emotions radiate to us. That is why it is so important to surround yourself with positive people rather than negative individuals in order to get in a good mood.

My daughter demonstrates this perfectly. She knows how to shift my energetic field. When she does something wrong, and I reprimand her, she will look down and put on a frown. Then she will look up, make eye contact with me, and flash me a cheeky little smile. It works every time. She shifts my energy from being angry to laughing (and she ultimately gets her way by helping to shift my mood).

Needless to say, your relationships with others can play a huge role in being in and sustaining your good mood. So many emotions circle around our love for others. I have found that it is important to stay self-aware and keep a close inner watch on those emotions because strong relationships will make you feel valued while poor relationships will have you questioning your self-worth and will help to keep you in a bad mood.

Once, I had been pining over the desired attention of a certain gentleman. He had made it known that he was unsure of his feelings toward me. And, yet, I continued to spend time with him when possible. I even caught myself from time to time during the day thinking about him romantically. At times, yes, this made me feel good, but the danger lay in when I snapped back to reality and was forced to contend with negative emotions. This pendulum swinging can be treacherous when it comes to your good mood. I am not saying that our emotions shouldn't swing from positive to negative throughout time. We are not static beings. But, absent a major event, the swinging should be more like the gentle rock of an unmanned hammock in the breeze as opposed to the recoil following a bungee jump.

Contrast my lovestruck daydreaming above with another relationship in my life – that of a dear friend. I spent time with her last night talking over all the wonderful and crazy events in our lives. She sends some tough but insightful words my way a lot of the time, but with her, I never feel the jerk of a recoil. With her, there is no doubt that she loves me and cares about my well-being. Even though she may disagree with me, my self-worth is never an issue. The relationship with her adds to my good mood and helps sustain it because I feel loved and valued consistently. These are the types of relationships to culti-vate. Any relationship that has you questioning your self-worth or self-confidence isn't going to help you regulate your mood. Those relationships only make the recoil that much harder to withstand.

Lately, I have turned to writing and public speaking as a means to send out love to others. I honestly do not believe any of my material comes from me, *per se*. I believe I express the creativity that is sent to me. Whatever comes out on paper or in words just happens to be my personal interpretation of those messages or thoughts coming from the Universe. These are, I believe, messages or thoughts that someone out there, other than myself, needs to hear. Maybe only one person out there needs to hear that specific message on any given day at any given time, but the hope is that through my voice, the message is received by the designated recipient.

My true desire in sending out these messages is to help others in any way I can, in perhaps a way that only I personally can help. I don't mean this to sound arrogant or conceited. I just know that the same message, delivered in a different way or by different people, has a very different effect on those who may be listening. I do not believe I am living in a bubble. Everything I do has consequences. Everything I do, in one way or another, touches someone else. I may never truly understand the full breath of how connected we all are, but I know we are connected. We are connected through our love for each other.

It is said that love is a bird with two wings – compassion and wisdom. I take my lessons learned and apply them to others' circum-stances. I send out love and await its return. Then I send it out again.

You have amazing power within you. You can shift the mood of another human being just by smiling at him or her, by hugging him or her, by touching him or her. Likewise, you can use human interaction to shift your own mood. Have a pleasant conversation with another. Give someone a hug or a peck on the cheek. Laugh with your children. Compliment someone. Accept a compliment from someone else. The point here is you do not have to rely solely on your own energy all of the time to get into a good mood and stay there. Acknowledge the other people around you – receive their good thoughts and gestures – and leave good energy with them. You will perpetuate the cycle and have an endless supply of good vibes.

> "Loving life is a two-way street… We don't receive care and compassion if we don't extend them to others."
> ~ *George Shinn*

CHAPTER 6

All Roads Lead to Rome (Spirituality)

"The spiritual road runs both ways."
~ Mischa V. Alyea

Your personal spirituality is your prime meridian.

You cannot make the leap to living on a higher frequency, i.e., getting into a better mood, without incorporating a spirituality practice into your daily routine and lifestyle. In order for anything to manifest or come to fruition, the idea must pass from the physical plane you inhabit into the realm of Universal intelligence. There is only one way this can happen – through a spiritual connection. All spiritual roads truly do lead to Rome, but you have to start down a road.

For me, the easiest means of connecting to a higher level is through meditation. Meditation is the means through which I attribute the majority of good in my life. Meditation has opened my soul to answers I thought I never would obtain and ideas I never thought possible. Meditation is the key that unlocks the treasure chest that is the Universe.

I meditate daily. I use it as a means to check in on my body, on my mind and on my spirit. You don't have to devote more than a few minutes each day to meditation and you don't have to be perfect in your practice. What I mean by that is, keep it simple. Focus on your breath. Focus on a mantra or affirmation. Focus on the quiet. Be still and listen to what the Universe has to say.

Scientific research has shown that by just taking a few moments every day to check in and focus on clearing your mind, you can reduce stress, anxiety and, yes, depression. It is a drug-free, cost-effective and simple way to establish balance in your life and elevate your mood. The more frequently you practice meditation, the more the effects sustain themselves throughout your day and throughout your life. Daily meditation practice equals daily sustained good mood.

This is a far-out concept for some people. Spirituality is different than intellect – it is something you must sense or feel to experience. The sight of someone sitting cross-legged, eyes closed in the middle of a city park at 2:30 pm on a random Tuesday has freaked more than one of you out. We aren't comfortable with the concept. We aren't comfortable with it because it has never been taught to us. And, as with anything that is uncomfortable to us, we resist it. I have heard every excuse from people about why they don't meditate – I can't do it; I don't have the time; That stuff is for hippies; My spouse will think I'm nuts; I can't still my mind, so why bother?; I have a bad back. (Seriously?) But meditation doesn't have to be a rigorous task. It shouldn't be painful or overly time-consuming. What it should be is meaningful over time. You must establish a meaningful connection with the Universe before anything will transpire.

The term "meaningful" is different for everyone. I know my connection with the Universe has been meaningful for me when I feel as though I have given the Universe something, usually in the form of gratitude, and the Universe has given me something in return, usually in the form of an idea, a light feeling or mood, or in the form of a connection with another part of the Universe. Not every single meditation session will yield this for me, and not every time I am given a gift is it with the same intensity. Sometimes, the Universe feels very still. Other times, I can't keep up with everything it is throwing at me. I do my best to quiet my mind so that when the Universe calls, I am ready to listen and, if need be, respond through action.

I believe that when I tap into the Universal energy around, my desires are handed over to me. I didn't even need to do any work. All I had to do was tap in and listen. And magically, things appear in my mind in the form of wants. If I stay with these ideas long enough, and put more energy into them, they morph into desires, and eventually, if fed properly, into life obsessions. The Universe always wants what is best for me. The Universe always wants for me what I want for myself. The Universe works magically, flawlessly and tirelessly to set into motion what we ask of it. The trick lies in mastering how to ask for the right things instead of things we don't want, and then, in staying the course.

When the Universe gives me an idea, I treasure it. I may elect to keep it or pass it on to another soul, but I know that at that very moment, the Universe has entrusted me with something very precious. And when those precious items land with me and stir deep emotion inside me, I know that the spark of desire has been born, and it is up to me to nurture and fan the flame.

> "Your Soul is your ultimate guidance system.
> You can think of your Soul as the compass, map, and destination, all in one."
>
> ~ Aletheia Luna

CHAPTER 7

Get a Move On (Exercise)

"Habituate yourself to walk very far."
~ Thomas Jefferson

You need to physically move. So, put your butt in gear!

I'm not kidding. Your attitude consists of more than just your mind – your body is involved. When you are moving, you are expanding. When you are sedentary, you are shriveling. I had forgotten this lesson for a brief time, and it cost me substantially.

At one point in my life, I had become very unhappy. For the longest time, I ignored my feelings. However, there was always one thing about me that, throughout my life, served as a barometer for my mood. That was my weight. I could not ignore my weight – the scale does not lie.

Then it came – chronic illness. I started exhibiting bizarre and inexplicable symptoms. I went to numerous doctors, all of whom were perplexed, until I was finally diagnosed with an inflammatory arthritis autoimmune disorder.

So, as you can see, my bad mood was costing me more than I was willing to pay. After dealing with some pretty scary medications, I made some very drastic changes in diet and got off the medication. But I did not shift my fitness level, and so, I continued on carrying around a lot of extra baggage. As much as I would like to blame outside forces, this was, again, all on me.

Then one day, I woke up. I realized my daughter was watching me. How could I ever expect her to take care of herself if I couldn't show her how? So, I signed up and walked into a nearby CrossFit gym, terrified and having no idea what to expect. And while I eventually fell in love with both the training and the people, the beginning was hard.

I remember going to CrossFit class one evening, very early on, and being told that the warm up was 500 meters on the rower. I was not a good rower. I got on and started, and the coach came over and said, "You (he didn't know my name yet), just row 300 meters, okay?" It was obvious to him that it was going to take me a long time to get to 500 meters. A few seconds later, when everyone was getting off their rowers, the coach said to me, "Just do 200." I was mortified. I almost didn't go back after that night. I went home and soaked in the tub hoping and praying that I could move my body in the morning.

But, my desire outweighed my habit to continue on as I was, so right then, I made another decision. I told myself that I would do CrossFit for three months. I would fully commit for that long. If I didn't like it after that, I could stop and find something else. I also told myself I had to go more than three times a week during those three months. It was one of the hardest things I ever did – not even from a physical standpoint but from a mental one – but I continued with my actions. I made it past that three-month mark and kept going.

Then, one day, in the middle of a workout with about 8 million burpees in it, I started paying attention and said to myself, "Um, hey, who is this girl? When did she show up? She's getting pretty good at this stuff." I couldn't do a year ago what I can do today. And that means growth has occurred. Not growth I can measure like a waist size – although my measurements have gone down – but growth of my spirit and my mind.

But you know the most important benefit? That's right, my mood shifted. I was actually having fun while my butt was being kicked. I woke up in a better mood and sustained a better mood throughout the day. My daughter and I started singing together in the car. We had more fun playing and running outside together. As my mood elevated, my weight went down at a pretty rapid rate. And while I know CrossFit burns a lot of calories, the real reason the weight dropped off so fast is because I was in a place where I no longer needed to carry it – I was – happy. And for me, that's the greatest reason to keep going.

You don't need to be an elite athlete to benefit from movement. Try walking outside, playing with your kids, yoga, tai chi. The possibilities are almost endless. I could have picked any number of ways to get moving, but the most important thing was I got moving, and my movement continues to pay dividends in the form of a good mood.

> "An inch of movement will bring you closer to your goals than a mile of intention."
>
> *~ Steve Maraboli*

CHAPTER 8

Travel Companions (Find the Like-Minded)

"Surround yourself with like-minded people who support you on the road to success."
~ Shirley George Frazier

Sometimes, being yourself is hard work.

There are a lot of people out there with their own opinions of who we should be. As a result, we tend to walk in the middle of the road rather than lean to one side or the other. When we don't pick a side and instead elect to go along with the crowd, we think we are less likely to offend people and more likely to fit in.

I spent a lot of time living with and surrounding myself with people who were not like-minded. I've spent a great portion of my life with people who were always in bad moods.

I was actually convinced at one point that the reason I had fallen into a depression in the first place was because I had attempted to be my own self. The depression was punishment for not carrying the burden I was meant to bear throughout life, for not sticking to the straight-and-narrow and for not going with the flow. So, when I finally got out of the haze and set my sights on law school, I also set my sights on being as "normal" as everyone else.

I made sure to dress like everyone else and to sound like everyone else. I convinced myself that I wanted the same career goals as everyone else. I graduated and entered the workforce determined to work hard and climb the ladder like everyone else. Luckily, I loved the law. I liked thinking about it, weighing the pros and cons, developing arguments, and I loved advocating for my clients. What I did not like was the profession. I did not enjoy arguing constantly for the sake of arguing and mostly over things of little significance.

So, given my career and relationships as they were, I was left with only one option if I was ever going to be happy – I needed to seek out and spend time with individuals who thought like me. In fact, I needed individuals who thought bigger than me. I needed a real mentor.

This was a difficult thing for me to admit. I had looked for a good mentor most of my life. Many people didn't have the time or the inclination. I didn't know where to start, but the point is, I just had to start somewhere.

When you are searching for answers to hard questions, it means a lot to have someone wiser to engage with. Once I started interacting with like-minded people, my life drastically changed. I was in an environment where I was not only encouraged to be who I wanted to be, but I was also accepted and appreciated for it. The more encouragement I received, the farther I dug into who I am and who I have the potential to become. I became braver and found the courage to change the things in my life that no longer made me happy.

Granted, there were a number of people who did not understand my need to change, nor did they like or approve of it, but this time I did not bow to the pressure because I had mentors and friends helping me through the process. Instead of retreating, I continued to follow my heart. I continued to look for the real me.

And when I found her, I found her carrying with her the most remarkable good mood.

So, don't feel as though you have to go it alone. But you do have to take your own path. Be true to yourself. Find the like-minded. And then, as I have said to my daughter, follow your heart and the rest will follow you.

> "We travel, some of us forever,
> to seek other states, other lives, other souls."
> ~ *Anais Nin*

CHAPTER 9

Put Yourself on the Map (Your Self-Image)

*"Low self-esteem is like
driving through life with your hand-brake on."
~ Maxwell Maltz*

How you see yourself is everything.

I don't know too many people who don't have some self-image issues. Maybe two or three people at the most. These people are so secure in who they are and what they do that absolutely nothing fazes them: not what they are wearing, not how their body looks, not how they sound when speaking, not whether their message will empower some and bother others. Think about that for a moment – what an incredibly freeing feeling it must be to truly not care about what anyone else thinks because you are so secure in knowing your true self that others' opinions simply don't matter. It takes a lot of self-awareness work to get there, but I think the destination is so worth it.

However, right now, I sometimes suffer from self-image issues. I know this is true because where I want to be and where I am are two different places on the map. It's like those times when you know you put in the correct address of a destination into your GPS, but you end up somewhere that isn't even close to where you had wanted to go. I hate when that happens.

So, first there's the "easy" part of this issue. There is the physical, body-image issue that most of us suffer from, yes even you dudes out there. Personally, I find it a little hard to scroll through Instagram and look at model after model, touched-up photo after another and not start to judge how I look in comparison. I think this starts as a natural reaction. I also think this initial reaction isn't necessarily bad. Comparison is necessary in some respects of life. It is helpful for me to look at two different people and compare them to determine their identity. It is also helpful to be able to distinguish loved ones in a crowd of people. So, comparison is necessary. It helps us on a social level. It helps us survive.

I also don't think this initial comparison reaction is bad when I use it constructively. I sometimes spend a fair amount of time at my CrossFit gym. While I'm there, by human nature, I spend a lot of time looking at bodies, and quite frankly, I am mostly looking at the women. I know where I am on my fitness journey and where I want to be. When I see others who have already achieved what I wish to achieve, it makes me continue to work toward my goals because I see what is possible. Again, I don't think this is a bad thing. Where this turns into harmful behavior is when I start saying negative things to myself about how I look presently. This is just self-destructive and serves no purpose.

I have spent many years in the past not liking myself. It took a lot of work for me to begin liking myself again. And once I liked myself, I started learning how to love myself. Once in a while, I still find it hard to focus on the good points of myself rather than my perceived flaws, but I am proud to say I waste less and less time focusing on the negative or on things I simply cannot change.

You will never reach any of your goals if you first can't imagine yourself reaching them. And you can't imagine yourself reaching them if your self-image – both the physical and the mental side of it – doesn't match that of the person imagined. Love yourself for what you have to offer and for who you are becoming. Your attitude about yourself and your present life depends on it.

Great, you're thinking, but how do I make this change to loving myself – all of myself? These ideas you carry around about yourself won't just fall out of your head or change overnight. Again, I think it takes a great level of self-awareness to break the cycle and shift the mindset. First, and this is a concept I talk about and teach about a lot, I need to accept the present – this is who I am and how I look right now. This is a fleeting moment in time – a snapshot of my overall life. How I look today will not be how I look three months from now nor is it how I looked three months ago. My body and my mind are always works in progress. There is always something I can improve upon, but that doesn't mean I should take away from what I have today. I am healthy. I am smart and I am strong. So, promise to accept yourself for who you are today.

Next, I have to understand where the comparison comes from and then stop it before it gets to be destructive. The only real comparison of any value on your good mood journey is that with your former self. Promise to work on the things you can and want to change about yourself for the better. Also promise to let go of the things you cannot change – things you have no control over.

The last part of self-awareness is the biggest and most important part. I think self-image is a mental *and* a spiritual issue. I actually think it is more spiritual. It comes from who I am on a deeper level than just what I *think* about myself. It comes from what I *believe* about myself.

What does it mean to believe in something – in some idea or some concept? What does it mean to know something so well and so deeply that no outside influence or opinion can make you feel any differently? Belief is the most powerful concept behind your good mood journey because when we believe, our self-image changes into a picture of that person we want to become. And then, we become that new person. Belief means we are not attached to how others respond to us because we know how we feel about ourselves, and that is enough. Belief means that we can attain anything we desire. Belief means we have the power to change ourselves and the world.

But what do you do until you raise yourself to the level of belief? Fake it till you shake it, baby! Fake your behavior until you are able to shake that old image of yourself completely.

Sometimes, the idea of getting and maintaining a good mood seems insurmountable. You couldn't flip that switch in your mind from negative to positive if you had a two-hundred-pound magnet. It's frustrating. It's tiring. It is sometimes agonizing and debilitating. And, as I said before, it just plain sucks.

You know what to do when you find your gas tank on empty, right? You get out and push. You create an alternative means of propulsion until you reach the nearest gas station.

Forward movement is movement regardless of how slow you are going, regardless of how many pistons are firing, regardless of how many other cars speed past you. Try faking it for a while. It will at least get you moving.

Ah, yes, but what does faking it look like? I would start with creating a picture in your mind of who you want to become. When you are firing on all cylinders, what does that look like? How do you dress, how do you move, how do you talk, what music do you listen to? Take these ideas and fake them. Dress like you would if you were in a good mood. Listen to that upbeat, lift-you-up song. Wing your eyeliner and strut your stuff. *Pretend* to be in a good mood.

When you pretend, a number of things happen. First, there is a chemical response in your body. Scientific research has shown that just by placing a smile on your pretty, little face you can elevate your mood, boost your immune system and possibly even lower your stress level. All that reward just for doing something as easy as faking a smile with your facial muscles. You don't even have to really mean it.

Next, the longer you pretend to be or feel something, the more you start to internalize that feeling into your subconscious mind. If the faking becomes a habit, you will find that your subconscious eventually will take over and you won't have to pretend anymore. The actions and feelings will be automatic and ever-present. They will become part of you. No more faking required.

I once went after a job that, at the time, I felt was a little out of my league. Much to my surprise, I crushed the interview and got hired on the spot. I was in real trouble. I had managed to fake my way through the interview, but how, oh how, was I ever going to fake my attitude for the duration of end-to-end work weeks? I thought I was doomed.

The weekend before my start date, I was panicking. I could feel the nausea starting to set in. But I really wanted this job. And deep down, I knew I was competent and qualified for it. So, I made myself get up and leave the house. I got a new haircut, got my nails done (which I rarely do), bought a new suit and a couple of pairs of killer business heels. I got ready that Monday morning determined to show them what they had invested in was well worth it. I faked my attitude, my mood and my way through the first week…and then the second…and, yes, then the third…but by the time the fourth week rolled around, I was still getting my nails done *and* I no longer felt like a fraud. The "fake" personality I had been trying on was sticking. I was becoming that confident woman I thought I wasn't. The truth was, I was that woman all along. I just didn't believe it.

Pretending showed me that you can, over time, develop the attitude you want to have. You can change your mindset, your mood and thus, your life, in a very short period of time. (And, as long as you keep it your own little secret, no one will ever know you were faking it.)

So, here's to getting to the level of believing. Here's to believing, to knowing from the inside-out that we are beautiful, smart, courageous, important, worthy, strong and loved – all the things I make my daughter tell herself in the mirror before bed. Because I know that when that inner monologue of yours hits the level of belief on a positive level, you will be unstoppable.

> "Whatever course you decide upon, there is
> always someone to tell you that you are wrong.
> There are always difficulties arising
> which tempt you to believe that your critics are right.
> To map out a course of action and follow it
> to an end requires… courage."
> *~ Ralph Waldo Emerson*

CHAPTER 10

Put the Wind Back in Your Sails (Daily Rituals and Self-Care)

*"Motivation is what gets you started.
Habit is what keeps you going."*
~ Jim Ryun

Positive daily living – the *sine qua non* of a sustainable good attitude.

There are a lot of activities that you can make part of your daily ritual that serve to help sustain a good mood. And while not all of these may seem exciting or groundbreaking, they are some of the most important things you can do to support your mental health, your mood and your spirit.

A great place to begin when talking about rituals, positive triggers and holding a better attitude or mood is to get a clear picture of who you are and what you stand for. I achieved this by creating, solidifying and writing down a list of my core values, which I review often.

If someone asked you for a list of your core values, could you give it to them? You may think you know what is fundamentally important to you, but if you haven't spent the time really thinking about it, chances are you can't be crystal clear about them and easily articulate them. Take this opportunity now to develop a strong and concise list of core values for yourself. There are many exercises you can use to discover your list. I don't have a preference of how you get there; just get there. My list includes: bravery (courage), love, integrity, nature, diligence, wisdom, appreciation (gratitude), growth (expansion), enjoyment (fun) and respect. This spells out the acronym BLIND WAGER. With this said, I never forget my core values and can rattle them off at the drop of a hat. A "blind" bet or wager, in the gambling world, is when you place your opening bet in order to enter into the pot and play a hand. In other words, a blind wager is the faith and courage to give yourself a chance.

Why are core values so important to me? They serve as my compass. I immediately know when I'm headed into a depressive cycle of thinking. I start feeling edgy, squirrely, anxious. I get that itch to run away even when I have no idea from what I am running. Before, I used to sit in this feeling and allow it to intensify until I could no longer control it. Now, when that feeling shows up, I start paying attention. I now know that when that feeling inside me arises, one (or more) of my core values is not being honored in some way. I immediately stop, close my eyes, take a deep breath and shine the light inward to see what might be going on. Emotions are chalk-full of great information – kind of like the dashboard on your car. Don't avoid them. Use them to your advantage.

Small steps can make a huge difference as long as you stick with them. There are a number of other practices I slowly picked up as time went on, which were easy to do every day but also made a huge difference. We are inundated daily with stimuli. Our minds become fatigued, and our mood suffers as a consequence. Meditation, as discussed before, is a great daily ritual, and it allows for a chance to shut out the chaos of the world. Along those lines…

Consider turning off the television – at least for a while. I have barely watched television in almost two years. I also cut out the news and random browsing of the internet and I limit time on social media. This was in response to that squirrely feeling. I learned quickly that when I eliminated these unnecessary distractions, I was less angry. Then I became happier and more peaceful. Trust me – if something important enough in the world happens, you *will* hear about it. I now go to the internet only for targeted information I need.

In all honesty, I could no longer handle the constant barrage of bad news, stories of pain and instances of lack that the media forces upon us. On the other side of the coin, many television shows were making me feel less than. I was jealous and television was making me feel small. I needed to fill my mind with ideas of size. So, now I read books, and I read a lot of them. Not trashy novels, mind you, but books of substance with the intent to learn something. I cannot express to you what a profound effect this had on my life. I don't even miss the television. In fact, when it is on, I feel a little squirrely.

Journaling is a great daily exercise for the mind and soul. I find this exercise useful when that squirrely feeling shows up and I am having a hard time pinpointing the cause. Taking the time to sit down and write is one of the best things you can do for yourself. Your writing doesn't need to have a direction or a solid purpose. Just write and see what comes up for you. You may be surprised by what your soul is trying to tell your mind.

And then, there is laughter. If you aren't laughing every day, you aren't really living.

One thing I seemed to have inherited from my father is a good sense of humor. I sometimes lose sight of this and this is a dangerous tool to lose because if you can't take a joke once in a while, well then, I'm afraid the joke is on you. Sharing a sense of fun and levity with others can be healing, bring people together and help maintain an elevated mood.

When we were young, my brother and I grew up mainly at our father's boarding stable, a place where many pranksters kept their horses. One day, to get back at the chief culprit, a group of women teamed up and sought their playful revenge. They took the man's white horse out of its stall and proceeded to paint its coat with rainbow-inspired polka dots – pink, green, blue. When the man showed up, he never even flinched. He saddled up his horse like any other day and took it out for a trail ride. Of course, later on he admitted that he found it to be pretty funny.

I can tell you this much, those of us spectators had a hearty laugh when he rode off over the hill. It's a story that lives on today and still makes us chuckle every time we think about it.

Laughter has been scientifically proven to elevate your mood, reduce stress, boost your immune system and promote creativity. I think the best evidence of this is in watching children at play. They are almost always laughing at something. They dance and sing and laugh for no reason at all, all the while propagating that pleasantness of childhood and using their vivid imaginations.

You could stand to bring a little of that child-like state back into your life. Laugh. Really laugh. Tell silly stories. Watch funny movies. Banter in true witty fashion. Commit a harmless prank or two. Lighten the air around you, and in turn, lighten your overall mood.

Additionally, I highly recommend adopting a daily gratitude practice. Since gratitude is one of my core values, it should come as no surprise to you that I dedicate a small portion of my day, every day, to focusing on gratitude. This does not need to be complicated. In fact, it can be as simple as just sitting and jotting down a list of some of the things that you are grateful for in the present moment.

Other teachers encourage us to write down things we want to happen as if they have already happened, in the form of present gratitude. An example might be me writing down that I am grateful for this book reaching hundreds of thousands of people and helping them find their good moods. There is a reason for this. When you are feeling a sense of gratitude, you are in an incredibly high state of vibration. If you are thinking about what you want while in this state, you have greater potential of realizing that which you desire. This is where dreaming enters the picture, which we will discuss a little later.

And speaking of core values and gratitude… for me, being outside is pivotal to maintaining a good mood. During the winter months, I notice a change in my behavior, and eventually, in my mood if I do not venture outdoors. I would never make it to spring if I didn't force myself to spend time outside to stave off the looming seasonal blues.

It is imperative that I breathe fresh air, see the sky and witness natural light. I need to touch green grass with my bare feet every-so-often and feel the wind on my face. I also love sleeping outside whenever I can.

Interestingly enough, I also have an inexplicable affinity for the ocean. I see this pull, this attraction, even greater in my daughter. Every time I step foot on a beach and witness the rolling waves, I cry as if I am returning home after a long time away. The sight instantly fills my soul with love and beauty that is unmatched by any other experience.

Then there are a vast number and type of goal reminders and other positive triggers that I use. In my bedroom, on the wall opposite to my bed, I have hung several things. One thing hanging there is a big white board. On this white board, I have written out my goals. Immediately below my white board, I have hung a number of different vision boards, each with its own sort of theme. Interspersed throughout all this, I have hung many quotes and drawings that trigger some kind of positive emotional reminder for me: items reminding me of inspiration, courage, fortitude, patience, balance, desire, etc.

This wall is the first thing I see when I wake up in the morning and the very last thing I see before I close my eyes at night. When I wake up, it serves as an immediate trigger – get up, get going, go after what you want – everything you dream of is right in front of you. How can you start your day in a bad mood with that in your face from the word "go"? Before bed, these are the last messages and images ingrained in my subconscious prior to sleep, so my mind is working at believing that everything I want is already within my reach.

More importantly, on that wall and throughout my entire room, I have placed numerous pictures of my daughter. This serves as the ultimate motivator and good mood trigger. A trigger is nothing more than a reminder and seeing her little smile as soon as I wake up makes me beam with gratitude and love. Knowing that Mama needs to get up and do a good job for her, to provide for her and to serve as a good role model for her, lights a fire under my butt hotter than a firecracker lit at both ends.

The last important piece in this section is on developing a ritual of self-care. This piece sometimes takes a little work, but it is essential to your success. How can you possibly be in a good mood if you aren't taking good care of yourself?

I think about how much time I have spent in the past taking care of *other* people. I think about how many meals I have missed, how many times I didn't drink enough water or get enough rest. I told myself I did these things in service to others. I sacrificed to help others get what they needed – things like work deliverables, good meals, rest, etc. I always thought if I was pushing harder for longer that it would pay off. My sacrifice would be rewarded somehow – less work later maybe, maybe return of a favor, maybe someone telling me they loved me.

But, what really happened was the following: I got tired and worn down to the point of becoming really sick and then I gained weight. What happened is that people came to expect that crazy level of effort from me all of the time and I came to expect not having any time for myself. It was a never-ending cycle. And do you know what a prolonged period of self-neglect does to you? It erodes your confidence. It skews your self-image. It makes you respect yourself a little less. All those days that I thought that I was being strong, I was becoming weaker in every way imaginable.

I now know that in order to be a true help to anyone, I have to first take care of myself. I have to eat right and take the time to sit down and finish a meal. I need to carve out time to exercise. I need alone time for myself – to read, to meditate. I absolutely need to get enough sleep. In order to be an effective writer, coach, lawyer, podcast host, mother, citizen, friend, teacher – you name it, I have to be on my game. And staying on top of my game takes some effort, but it is definitely worth it.

I look at it this way – what would I say to my daughter if I saw her meeting others' needs before her own? If I saw her working herself to death? If I saw her trying to please people who can't be pleased? If I saw her sacrificing herself and her light? I would throw a freaking fit – that's what I would do. I would sit her butt down and give her a good lecture on why she needed to stop. I would talk to her about her health, her well-being, her self-image and her self-respect. And I would share with her the mistakes I have made so that she wouldn't be as ready to repeat them. So, if I would do that for my own daughter, and I know my daughter is watching me at every turn, then I absolutely need to do it for myself. And you, dear reader, you absolutely need to do it for yourself as well. Because if we won't take the time to take care of ourselves, to love ourselves, no one else will either.

So, love yourself like you are the love of your life! Adopt some new and inspirational daily rituals. And above all else, give yourself permission to have a little fun.

> "A person without a sense of humor is
> like a wagon without springs.
> It's jolted by every pebble on the road."
> ~ *Henry Ward Beecher*

CHAPTER 11

Tour of Duty
(Teach This Stuff to Others)

"Teaching is the royal road to learning."
~ *Jessamyn West*

Be a good listener. Be a teacher. Become a mentor.

After I had graduated from law school and gotten some time under my belt practicing law, I started teaching a few legal courses to undergraduates. My philosophy on teaching was that anyone could learn the material – I just had to figure out a way to explain it so that the students could absorb it. So, I would encourage students "to come talk to me before or after class if they were having trouble. What I found is that I ended up talking to a lot of them about more than the course. Many of the students wanted to talk to me about life… their academic careers… their professional careers… getting married… having children… moving to another country…signing a lease…buying a car… the list was endless. I had a number of students ask if I would serve as their academic advisor. Many begged me to have lunch with them or to advise them about upcoming assignments, exams or interviews. I became, much to my amazement, an immediate mentor – possibly by default – but one thing was made very apparent to me – these young men and women were as starved for a mentor as I once was.

Once I saw all this, I made it my mission to mentor those who sought out my help – even if I felt like I had little to give in the way of experience or advice; even if I felt like I didn't have the right answers; even if I was swamped; even if I was tired; even if I was a little envious; even if I just didn't feel like it. I created the time to do it because I remembered how much I once needed someone.

I wish someone in my early life had told me how short life really is and that it is worth being happy. I wish that someone in my young life had talked to me about following my heart. I wish someone told me to go after my dreams with everything I had. I wish someone told me at one point they believed in me. Maybe then, I would have believed in myself at an earlier age, and perhaps avoided some of the mistakes I made. And maybe not. The past is no longer of great importance to me, except for what I learned, and that is that people need to be mentored. People need others to encourage them and believe in them. People need to see different perspectives while they are young. People need to know the truth about what is out there and then, armed with the truth, know that they have the ability to achieve in spite of it – if they are willing to put in the work, the time and the effort.

I teach and mentor for the benefit of others, but I am the one who truly benefits. There is no greater reward than watching someone you have mentored go out there and crush it! More than that, if you want to learn something on a deeper level, teach it. Every time I discuss some of these concepts with someone else, I learn a little more. I can then go and implement the learning in my own life. Keeping my good mood gets a little easier each time I uncover a new way of explaining how to do it to someone else.

My dear reader, here is my plea to you today. Go out and mentor. Look for people who want a mentor but are too shy to ask. Mentor those who ask and who give you good reason to mentor them.

Mentor on your profession, on your life experience, on your current situation and mentor on how to get into and how to stay in a good mood.

This much I know, dear reader. The more you teach others about being in a good mood, the more you learn about keeping yourself in a good mood. Teach to learn and grow yourself. Mentor for the sake of your own good mood.

> "Learning is like rowing upstream;
> not to advance is to drop back."
> ~ *Chinese Proverb*

CHAPTER 12

Rite of Passage
(Pay Close Attention to Your Habits)

*"One recognizes one's course by
discovering the paths that stray from it."*
~ Albert Camus

Take care of how you live your life. The effects will take care of themselves.

Your mood is the state of mind wherein everything around you is created. That's why I am careful with my rituals, triggers and how I view myself.

So, if your attitude is your creative state, then the best indicator of whether you are on track is the results you see coming into your life. If you don't like what is coming to you, chances are you need to shift your attitude. As a lawyer, I might describe this phenomenon as a causal link, and the evidence of this link is as strong as the force of the Universe itself.

But, while you should always be paying attention and noticing your results, focusing on the effects themselves is fruitless and, quite honestly, exhausting. You can't control anything in this Universe –

not one single thing or being – other than yourself. Put your mind power on yourself and keep it there.

Looking back, whenever I was truly successful at anything, a similar block of time preceded that success. This period of time consisted of putting my nose down and plowing through, with focus only on the tasks at hand and little else. This was how I made it through my depression, through law school and the beginning of my legal career, through a bout with autoimmune disease and through my divorce. It is also how I manifested all of the good in my life. Shoulders back, nose down, eyes forward. I have no doubt that this philosophy will continue to help me. (Potty training, anyone?)

The problem with this philosophy, though, and with this preceding block of time, is that it is not sexy. There is little to grab and hold your attention, little positive feedback, lots of external criticism and little variety. That's why I have found it helpful to lose myself in it. Habit must take over. Your willpower will surely fail you.

These are the times in my life when my mother and my mentors tell me I look unattractive – the times when I go way too long without a haircut, when I haven't updated my wardrobe for quite some time, when I don't have a clue as to what month it is and when a little eyeliner would go a long way. Time becomes irrelevant, because quite honestly, every day the focus remains the same.

This time period is hard if you don't have a plan in place. It's hard because you aren't getting immediate results. You are working on the only thing you can control, which is yourself. You are working on the cause. But when the effects start becoming apparent, when the desired results come, they are usually pretty remarkable. And that's when you know your attitude is on track – when your thoughts match that which you seek to achieve.

A good reminder of this concept, for me, is in watching baseball. I never paid much attention to this idea until I watched my brother play one afternoon in a college game. He hit a home run that day, and while I saw a pleased expression come across his face when that ball went over the fence, he immediately dropped his head and ran the bases with focus and humility. Ever since that day, I watched how many of the pros actually did the same thing. Those "homerun" players who were working hard every day, whose talent was something earned, almost always did because what they and my brother all knew was there was always more work to be done. They were keeping good habits.

I give you the same advice that I give and will continue to give to my daughter. Drop your nose to your goals, but drop your chin to no one. Put some of these good mood habits into place and keep your eye on your desired prize – your ultimate good mood and an amazing life!

> "A man of ordinary talent will always be ordinary,
> whether he travels or not;
> but a man of superior talent will go to pieces
> if he remains forever in the same place."
> ~ *Wolfgang Amadeus Mozart*

CHAPTER 13

Blaze a Trail
(Be an Unbridled Dreamer)

"I haven't been everywhere, but it's on my list."
~ *Susan Sontag*

To win big, you have to dream big.

Your imagination is the gateway to your good mood and, ultimately, to your ideal life. You have the amazing ability to form the picture of any life you want and, by so imagining it, then living the life you desire. When your mood is dark and small, so is your world.

When I was a little girl, my dad would ask me what I wanted for Christmas. I used to tell him that I wanted magic. His response to me was that I already had it. I didn't understand what he meant at the time, but I sure do now. I have the magical ability to dream up anything I want and, *at the very same time*, the ability to eliminate anything from my life that does not serve me. The problem with our society is that, once we reach a certain age, we stop dreaming. In fact, dreaming is discouraged. The same man who told me I already had magic also told me a few years later that I could not change the world, that I would never have what others had and that

I only had the ability to achieve a certain level but nothing more. He also told me (and taught me) that I probably would never be truly happy. These were his beliefs, but after hearing them often enough, they soon became mine. Without even being aware of it, I gave up on anything that seemed slightly out of reach. I gave up on ever being happy.

To dream is to see color in your life. Otherwise, life is dull and gray. The outline of your life is there, but there is no vibrancy. Dreaming is what brings excitement into life, what makes it worth getting out of bed every morning.

When I went through my spiritual depression, I spent a lot of time lying around in bed. I had little energy most of the time and, quite frankly, I slept a lot in order to avoid the pain. My life consisted of little more than merely existing. I allowed my circumstances to dictate my attitude and that just turned into a vicious cycle. What I was lacking at the time was the knowledge of how important dreaming is. Had I been dreaming, I think it would have been difficult for me to stay so depressed. When you dream, you have hope, and when you have hope, you see potential and a future.

To me, dreaming is being alive. The bigger and better I dream, the more I feel connected to the Universe. And the more I feel connected to the Universe, the happier I feel. These days, I carve out a set amount of time every day just to sit somewhere peacefully and dream. That's right – I just sit there and dream and dream and dream. My favorite place to dream is when I'm in the saddle riding my horse, but I spend a lot of time dreaming in my car too. Laugh if you must, but some pretty cool ideas have come out of those dreams. I dream about my career, what my new ranch will look like, new opportunities and about how much you, dear reader, are going to love this book. I set no boundaries in my dreaming – everything is fair game. There are no barriers. There are no disappointments. I mean, what's the sense of dreaming if you are going to play by the same old rules?

Carry with you the attitude of a dreamer. Never stop dreaming – even when things aren't going your way, even when you are sad or frustrated, even when others make fun of your dreams or try to squash them right in front of your eyes. Build an amazing picture in your mind and then make the causal link from your mind into your reality. Strive not to limit yourself in your dreams in any way. It is your right to dream big. Take what is yours. You deserve to be happy.

> "The real voyage of discovery consists not in seeing new landscapes, but in having new eyes."
>
> ~ *Marcel Proust*

CHAPTER 14

A Seasoned Traveler (My Faith in You)

> "Throughout the centuries there were men who took first steps, down new roads, armed with nothing but their own vision."
>
> ~ Ayn Rand

Faith will get you where you want to be.

Let's be frank here. Anyone can find a way to get into a good mood for a few moments. Buy a new outfit that screams confidence and wear it out. Eat some chocolate cake. Hug a friend. Flirt. Listen to a great song. Do something nice for someone else. Go bungee jumping for real. There are endless ways to get a rush of endorphins. The art is in sustaining that good mood over time. The real practice is in keeping a good mood at times when things are not going in your favor.

Sometimes, you just have to let go and have faith. Letting go can be tough, especially when our society is constantly looking for extraneous causes for misfortune, disease and poverty.

As I mentioned earlier, during my adult years, I began having some medical symptoms. It started out with intense knee pain and then spread to other joints. I was later diagnosed with autoimmune inflammatory arthritis. It doesn't matter what it was called. The concern was that it was taking over my life. Of course, knowing what I know now, I was doing all this to myself. I was unhappy and stressed in my life, and I was constantly focused on these feelings. My body was just responding to what my mind was creating.

I ended up on medication for autoimmune disorders. The medication seemed to help for a short time, but the condition continued to worsen. What's more is that I had considered wanting to have a child, and I knew that I could never do that on the medication nor could I raise a baby if I couldn't even take care of myself.

I don't know what sparked in me, but one day, I just got tired of it. I said, "No more." I said, "I am not going to be sick my whole life. I am going to be healthy." So, I made some radical life changes. I changed my dietary and exercise habits. I worked on my self-image to be in alignment with that of a healthy person. I changed my thinking habits. I told myself every single morning and every single night before bed that I was healthy. Not too long after that, I started feeling better. I made it years without any medication. Then I got pregnant. I haven't needed the medication since I made that important decision and followed through with the requisite action. In fact, I have no symptoms at all.

People keep saying the pregnancy changed my hormones and that is why I got better. But that doesn't explain how I made it medication-free for years before my pregnancy. I took a leap of faith and trusted that I could heal myself, and I did.

Within us lies a great reservoir of untapped potential and power. You have let the world tell you that you can only go so far or do so much, and now, you believe that. Change the belief in yourself. A changed belief will lead to a changed attitude. A changed attitude will lead to different (and better) results.

Do not doubt yourself. Do not doubt the Universe. Carry an attitude of faith in all you do and in all you are. You are the most powerful being in your own life. Use that power. Be proud of that power!

Let go of fear. Look toward the future. Love who you are.

Be well and dream big, my dear reader. I have great faith in *you*!

> "If we are facing in the right direction,
> all we have to do is keep going."
> ~ *Unknown*

AFTERWORD

Over the past 25 years, I have been asked dozens of times to write something like this for other authors and I have respectfully declined every request except for two – one for my dear friend and best-selling author TJ Hoisington and the second… for Dannie.

Dannie doesn't have the big brand or massive fan base that others have, she may not have dined with presidents or been interviewed by Oprah (yet!), but she has something far more important – far more critical. She has authenticity.

When I first met Dannie, my observations were driven primarily out of curiosity. She said all of the right things; she wanted to reach people, she wanted to have a sincere impact in people's lives, she wanted to share all she had learned – good and bad. But truth be told, I've had countless people express similar feelings and ideas to me. Sadly, most who make such bold statements rarely walk the talk or, at the very least, are willing to walk it long-term. Dannie is different. She does more than walk the talk. For Dannie, the desire and willingness to impact the lives of others is simply hard-coded into her DNA. It is who she is, to her core.

For me, personally, being exposed to Dannie and her eternal "good mood" is mood altering and triggers an immediate mindset adjustment! Every time I engage her in any conversation or interaction, I leave with the same thought – "I need my friends and kids to know Dannie!" She has that type of impact wherever she goes. She isn't flashy, she isn't seeking attention. She is sincere, and she is so authentically transparent.

I have never been more thrilled about a new book entering into the world as I am about the one you now hold in your hand. (Or maybe the one which is on your digital screen, LOL.) The principles and tools she shares are timeless, yet they seem so new, so different coming from Dannie's powerful perspective. It is written in a simple to absorb style that doesn't get bogged down in the weeds and she doesn't over-talk a point. (So refreshing.)

Within a couple of pages, you will be a fan of Dannie's, but by the time you complete this book, you will be a student. I realize everybody makes extreme statements about how something will "change your life," so I won't do that. What I will tell you is that when you complete this book, you will think differently, react differently and as you do so, you will find your mood increases, your enthusiasm for life, love and business expands and your level of overall happiness will increase significantly. Is that life-changing? I'll let you be the judge.

Troy Dunn
TV Personality
www.TroyDunn.com

Dannie is an author, attorney, coach, entrepreneur and podcast host who loves horses, traveling and learning. She spends her days finding ways to help those who aren't experiencing the most fulfilling version of their lives. Her greatest job and joy is serving as mom to an amazing little beacon of light and hope, her daughter, Carson.

You can check out Dannie's podcast, The Dannie De Novo Podcast, on Apple Podcasts, Google Play, Stitcher, iHeart Radio and Spotify or go to @danniedenovo on Instagram for more information.

For coaching sessions with Dannie, or for her online course, visit her at danniedenovo.com. And check out Dannie's farm-themed children's books and toys at www.littleredbarnbooks.com.

Dannie De Novo

Subscribe for free to
The
Dannie De Novo
Podcast
on Apple Podcasts,
Google Play, Stitcher,
iHeart Radio
and Spotify.

Made in the USA
Middletown, DE
08 September 2022